St Augustine's Abł ,

Julian Luxford

CONTENTS

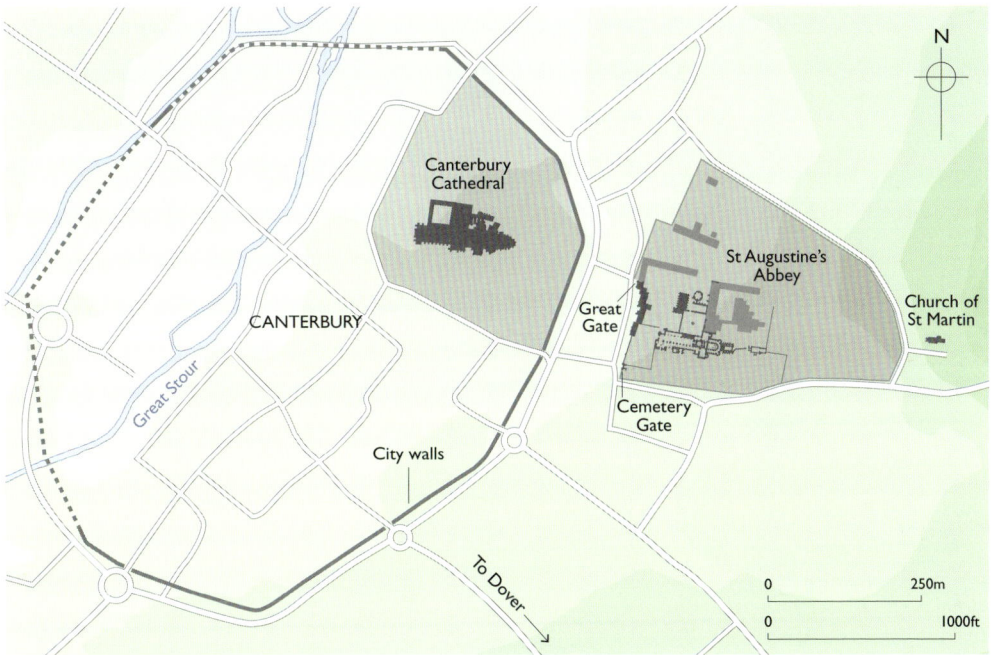

Tour of the Abbey

OVERVIEW AND SETTING

When Augustine and his party of missionary monks arrived in AD 597 at Canterbury, it was a decayed, flood-prone remnant of the Roman city it had once been. It was chosen, however, instead of London, because it was the seat of the powerful Kentish king Ethelbert (c.580–c.616), whose Frankish queen, Bertha, was already Christian, and who himself converted to Christianity, probably by 598. Canterbury was also readily accessible from Christian Gaul (France) and ideally placed to act as a station for religious expansion within England.

The abbey was built on the east side of Canterbury and, as it was to serve as a place of burial, just outside the city walls (bodies were not usually buried in centres of population for fear they would cause disease). Near the site was a pre-existing church that Augustine and his fellow missionaries used. This church, dedicated to St Martin and used by Queen Bertha and her Frankish chaplain Liudhard before Augustine arrived, still exists, although heavily rebuilt. Its earliest parts date to the sixth century.

Typically of a medieval monastery the abbey site comprised an inner precinct, with the main buildings and a lay cemetery, and an outer precinct, with vineyards, orchards and gardens. The whole was enclosed by a high wall both to guard and to symbolize monastic separation from secular life. The site was roughly wedge-shaped, tapering to the east, and about 500m on its longest side. There were two main gates in the west wall that followed the line of what is now Monastery Street.

Above: Map of Canterbury. The abbey's striking proximity to the cathedral would, as the power of the archbishops grew, prove problematic in the later Middle Ages
Below: The Church of St Martin, where Augustine and the early monks worshipped while their abbey church was being built

Facing page: Doorway in the north-west corner of the abbey cloister

Above: This baluster shaft, bearing the remains of polished limewash, came from a multi-light window, probably in the Church of SS Peter and Paul. It dates from the 10th or early 11th century

Below: Aerial view of St Augustine's Abbey remains from the south-east

A Site of the first church: Church of SS Peter and Paul

B Site of the second church: Church of St Mary

C Site of the third church: Church of St Pancras

D Site of Wulfric's rotunda

OVERVIEW OF THE CHURCH

A church, the spiritual engine room of any monastery, was the priority of Augustine and his fellow monks, and as soon as they settled in Canterbury in 597 they began to build one. The foundations of a porticus (side chamber) of this first church are visible north of the nave of the later Norman church.

Soon after the first church was built, a second, smaller church was built to its east, and in about 650 work began on a third still further east. Such an arrangement of structurally independent churches on an east–west axis was not unique (a similar one once existed at Glastonbury Abbey). At this time there was not the money, technology or reason for building large churches, so churches were added as and when required.

In the 11th century a large, octagonal structure was begun by Abbot Wulfric, joining the first and second churches. But soon after the Norman Conquest a new church more than 100m long was raised, replacing Wulfric's work and the two Anglo-Saxon churches it had linked. This cruciform building in the Romanesque style was variously altered over the next 400 years. The main addition identifiable today was a Lady chapel at the east end, built in the last phase of the Gothic style (the Perpendicular Gothic) in the late 15th and early 16th centuries and devoted to the worship of the Virgin Mary.

ANGLO-SAXON CHURCHES

Churches in Rome were built of stone, which is what Augustine and his royal patrons wanted for their English abbey. England then lacked a tradition of masonry construction (a skill that seems to have died out during the fifth or sixth centuries), so masons from Gaul were probably employed to create the first churches on the site. Besides timber, the main building materials available were flint, cement and secondhand Roman stones and bricks – all visible in the remains of the first church.

Left: Obverse of the 14th-century common seal of St Augustine's Abbey, showing Augustine enthroned between an unidentified archbishop and St Mildred, the first abbess of the nunnery at Minster-in-Thanet
Below: Initial from a near contemporary copy of Bede's eighth-century Ecclesiastical History. The portrait is probably of Pope Gregory I, although a later hand has written 'Augustine' in the halo

St Augustine of Canterbury

Within two years of setting off from Rome on his mission, St Augustine had baptized thousands of pagan English, including King Ethelbert of Kent.

Augustine of Canterbury (d.604) – not be confused with Augustine of Hippo (d.430), whose historical reputation is grounded in vast theological and philosophical scholarship – owes his fame to missionary activity and his status as first Archbishop of Canterbury. He was probably born in Rome (the year is not known) and while prior of the monastery of St Andrew in that city he accepted his mission from Pope Gregory I. Evidence of his character is slight, but the trust placed in him by the pope suggests a man thoroughly dependable, even charismatic.

In June 596 he left Rome for England with a party of monks. They got as far as southern Gaul when the alarm of his party over rumours of the hostility of the heathen English had him return to Rome for advice. Gregory encouraged him to persevere, made him an abbot and the missionaries set out again. On the way they were joined by monks from Gaul and the final party of 40 reached Thanet, Kent, in the spring of 597, where they parlayed with King Ethelbert.

Before long Augustine was leading a procession through the city of Canterbury,

displaying a silver cross and a painting of Christ and chanting a solemn litany.

He is said to have baptized thousands of pagan converts on Christmas day that year. He next devoted himself to establishing a cathedral within the city walls and an abbey outside to the east, and to trying, in the end unsuccessfully, to unite his mission with the Celtic Church in Wales (an organization, or group of organizations, that predated his mission and owed their existence to Irish missionaries).

St Augustine died on 26 May 604 and was buried in the abbey church when it was finished. A cult developed around his tomb and in 1091 his remains were moved to a glorious shrine at the east end of the church.

Top: Reconstruction drawing of the Church of SS Peter and Paul (left) and of St Mary (right) from the south-east, as they may have appeared in the eighth century
Above: An elaborately carved capital, dating from the seventh to the ninth centuries, possibly from the Church of SS Peter and Paul
Below: The graves of the third, fourth and fifth archbishops of Canterbury – Mellitus, Justus and Honorious – in the north porticus of SS Peter and Paul, under excavation in 1914–15

▮ Church of Saints Peter and Paul

The first church at the abbey was dedicated to SS Peter and Paul in 613. It was about 27m long and 18m wide with a gabled timber roof built that would have been either tiled or thatched. Towards the east end of the oblong nave may have been a pulpit and further east, probably set behind a low wall or screen with a central doorway, was the altar.

On either side of the nave were subdivided chambers (normal features of ambitious Anglo-Saxon churches), called 'porticus' by Bede and other early historians. The north porticus (later incorporated into the Norman church) was dedicated to St Gregory and contained the graves of the first six archbishops of Canterbury. Those of Mellitus, Justus and Honorius are visible in the north wall as small chambers where the coffins were set fast in pink cement; the shelter above them is modern. King Ethelbert, Queen Bertha and her chaplain Liudhard were buried in the south porticus, dedicated to St Martin. This porticus has not been excavated. The chancel at the east end, beyond the altar, took the form of an apse. It probably had seating for the clergy. At the west end, as was usual, was an antechamber, or narthex, which served as a station for processions and accommodated visitors who were not permitted further inside, such as those not yet baptized.

The church interior would have been dim. Construction methods at the time could not support large wall apertures, so windows and even reinforced doorways would have been small. Small windows, which were unglazed at this date, at least had the merit of keeping out the weather, and when shuttered would have blocked all natural light.

In 978 SS Peter and Paul was reconsecrated, the dedication to St Augustine added to that of the two apostles, and the church seems to have been partly rebuilt. While the extent of this work is unknown, it included the addition of a vestibule to the west, an outer porticus to the north and, possibly, some remodelling of the apse. It may have been at this date that the windows were first glazed. Small fragments of Anglo-Saxon glass excavated indicate that the first window glass was blue.

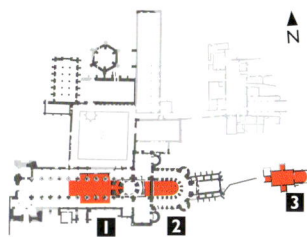

2 Church of St Mary

A short distance east of SS Peter and Paul stood the somewhat smaller Church of St Mary, dedicated to the Virgin Mary. The Mother of God was thought to merit her own church and its addition also provided more space for prestigious burials. It was built in about 620 by King Ethelbert's son and successor, Eadbald, who was buried there. This church was also oblong with porticuses to the north and south and an apsidal chancel (though none has been excavated as the building of the Norman church would have destroyed most traces of these remains). Only some footings of its west wall are now visible, pierced by a central doorway, to the east of Wulfric's rotunda.

3 Church of St Pancras

This church was of a similar size to SS Peter and Paul, but has survived better, having not been overbuilt after the Norman Conquest. It was oblong with an apsidal chancel, like the two earlier churches, and some 28m long, including its entrance porch. Part of the wall of this porch made of Roman brick survives. The construction and patronage of the church are undocumented, but it was probably begun in the mid seventh century, soon after the earlier churches. Probably in about 750 porticuses were added on the north and south sides, together with the west porch. Unlike the earlier two churches the nave

Above left: The Church of St Pancras from the south (1784), engraved after a drawing by Francis Grose. At this date it appears much of the western end of the church was still standing

Above: A lead coffin plate, probably from one of the graves in the monks' cemetery. It is inscribed Benedictus sacerdos *(Benedict the priest)*

Left: A reconstruction drawing of the Church of St Pancras seen from the south-east, as it may have appeared in the eighth century

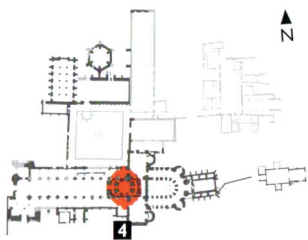

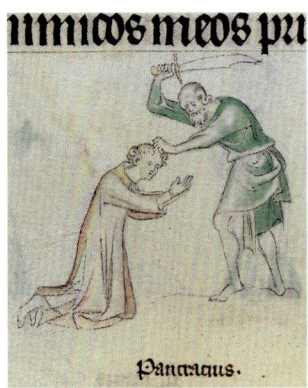

Above right: The Church of St Pancras from the north-west. The brickwork to the right is Anglo-Saxon, possibly part of the original seventh-century church, and is made of re-used Roman bricks

Above: A detail from an English manuscript of about 1310–20 showing the martyrdom of the 14-year-old St Pancras

and chancel were divided by a screen of columns and arches. Part of one column with a moulded base, made of imported French stone, remains in place on the south side.

In the late 14th century, when St Pancras's functioned as a cemetery chapel where special masses for the dead were celebrated, the apse was replaced by an oblong chancel with a large east window. The dedication to the early Christian boy-martyr Pancras is unusual. It was probably suggested by relics of this Roman saint that Augustine or a succeeding abbot brought to England. An early 15th-century chronicler of the abbey, Thomas of Elmham, who was for a short time its treasurer, says the dedication was chosen because appropriate to England, where the boys, according to Pope Gregory, looked angelic (as Pancras himself had appeared). Another chronicler, William Thorne, thought the church a pagan building consecrated to Christian use by Augustine himself. He tells a story of the saint expelling the devil from it and Elmham says the devil's claw marks are visible on the east wall.

4 Abbot Wulfric's Rotunda

The most unusual features of the ruins of St Augustine's are the foundations of an octagonal structure planned by Abbot Wulfric (r.1045–61) in the mid 11th century. They lie at the heart of the Norman church: the bases of eight wedge-shaped piers surrounded by an ambulatory, or gallery, and beyond that

a thick encompassing wall. There is nothing else quite like this in England and Wulfric surely realized that he was creating a distinctive, visually striking building. He evidently had an exemplar such as the octagonal basilica of San Vitale at Ravenna, Italy, a famous early Christian building of the sixth century, in mind. His idea was to link the Church of SS Peter and Paul to that of the St Mary and so form a single building, perhaps to create a more honorific setting for the tombs of the archbishops and kings.

Fortunately for posterity, his efforts are recorded by his contemporary, the monk and chronicler Goscelin of Canterbury (c.1035–c.1107). First, Wulfric demolished the east end of the Church of SS Peter and Paul and the west wall of the Church of St Mary, together with its western porticus. Work on the rotunda progressed as far as the arcade, or top of the first storey, before Wulfric fell ill and died in 1061, which Goscelin attributes to the Virgin Mary's displeasure at seeing her church mutilated. As often, one medieval abbot's pet building project did not interest his successors, and the rotunda was never completed. But, even if it had been completed, it would not have survived the ambitions of the Norman abbots who came after him for a vast, spatially integrated church.

Below left: A reconstruction drawing of the extended church with its rotunda, as it might have appeared in the mid 11th century had it been completed

A Tower
B Chapel
C Vestibule
D Narthex
E Church of SS Peter and Paul
F Wulfric's rotunda
G Church of St Mary

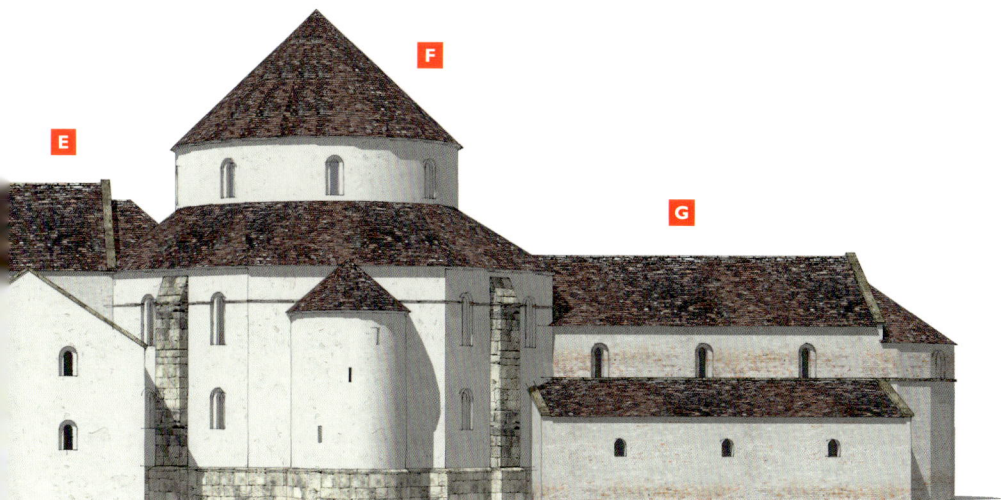

Gates of the Abbey

Above: *View of the Great Gate (c.1772–99) from what was the abbey's outer court, north-east of the gate. The little gateway to the left led between the inner and outer courts; by Benjamin Thomas Pouncey*

Below: *The Cemetery Gate from the west. It would have been used by monastic servants and for the admittance of bodies to be buried in the lay cemetery*

These two striking and formidable gates were intended to impress onlookers with the abbey's dignity and power.

The main gates between the monastery and the wider world were in the west wall, along what is now Monastery Street. In the 14th century these two gates were rebuilt, incorporating grand turreted gatehouses, with rooms over the entrance arches and porters' lodges to one side.

The larger of the two, built between 1300 and 1309 and called the Great Gate (or Findon Gate, after the abbot ruling at the time), is considered the most ambitious 14th-century ecclesiastical gatehouse in Europe. It was designed by the master mason Michael Canterbury (fl.1275–1321), a native of Canterbury who also worked at the cathedral priory. A royal licence to fortify the Great Gate with battlements was obtained by the monks in 1308.

The Great Gate established a model adopted for English gatehouses until the end of the Middle Ages. Its outer face was once adorned with sculpted figures and the top-heavy turrets are calculated expressions of institutional power. The internal façade, now faced with flint, but originally of freestone like the outer façade, was always less ornate.

Towards the end of the 14th century the second of the abbey's main gates, about 100m south of the Great Gate along the west wall, was

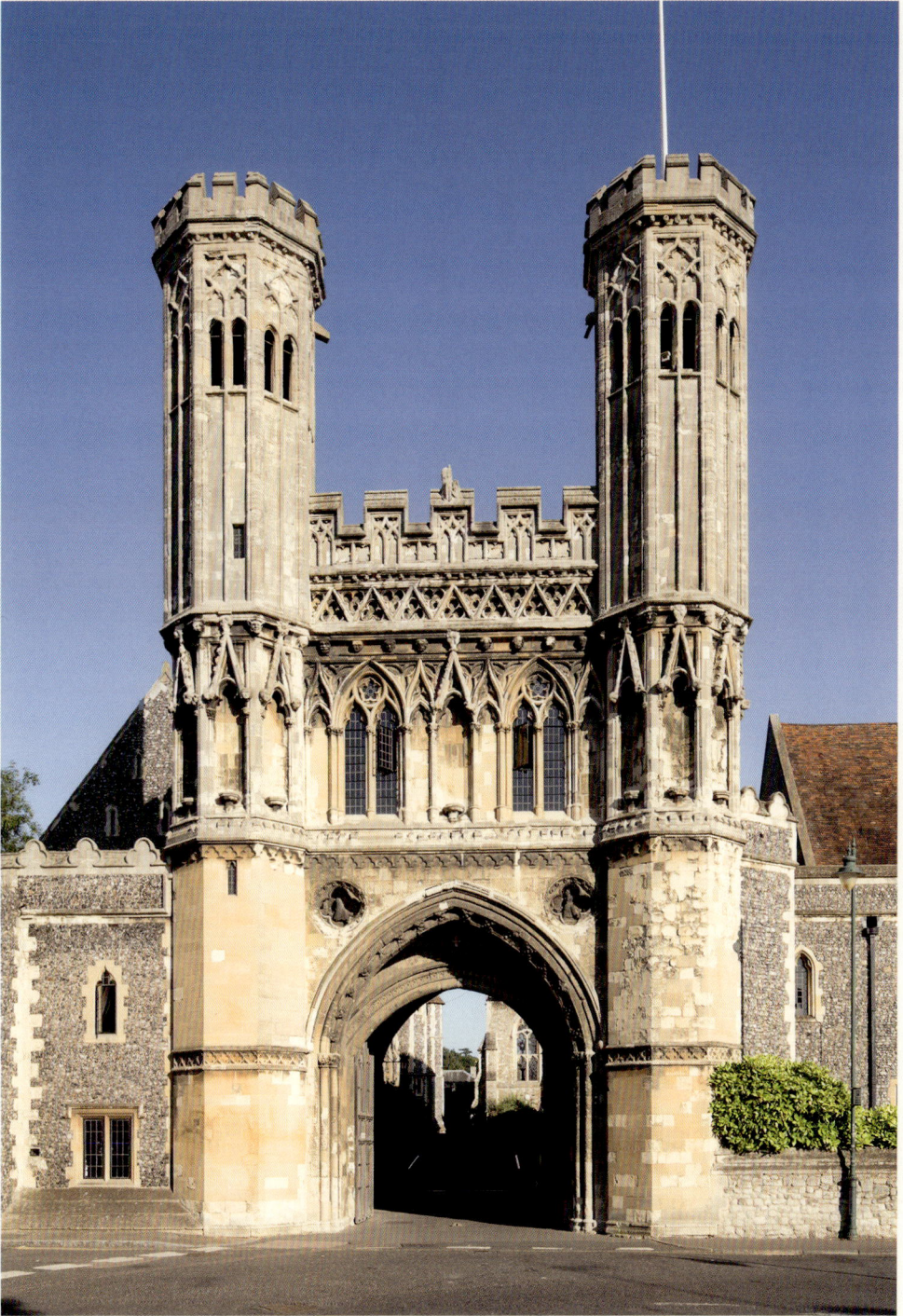

rebuilt. The building of the Cemetery Gate cost 660 marks. Although not as ornate as the Great Gate it has similar military airs and incorporates an overtly defensive feature: machicolations (slots between the corbels of the outer parapet through which defenders could project missiles at attackers below). As it happens the apertures were always blocked, but appearances were what mattered.

Above: The Great Gate from the west. The niches halfway up each turret would once have held statues

5 NORMAN CHURCH

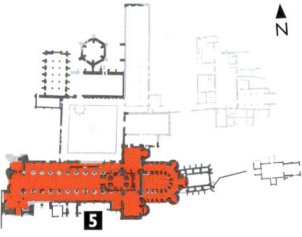

After 1066 William the Conqueror put Norman churchmen in
charge of England's major religious institutions. Their zeal for
church rebuilding and enlargement is astonishing. They were
rich, acquainted with architectural progress abroad, and able to
get the best master masons and finest stone from Normandy.
Within 40 years of the Conquest both the abbey church and
the cathedral at Canterbury were rebuilt in the 'Norman' style
of Romanesque, so-called for its place of origin and the patrons
responsible for its spread in England. These two buildings were
at the forefront of developments in structural engineering and
aesthetics, not just in England but across northern Europe.

Work of Abbot Scolland

Work at the abbey began at the east end in about 1073 and
probably concluded with the west front and its two towers in
the first decade of the 12th century. Once again, Goscelin of
Canterbury is a valuable source of information, and much can
be also inferred from the surviving remains. The instigator was
Abbot Scolland (r.1070–87), originally a monk of Mont Saint
Michel in Normandy. He employed an experienced designer
named Blitherius, whose skill Goscelin praises highly, and
arranged for building stone to be shipped from Normandy
(stone was also procured from Quarr on the Isle of Wight).

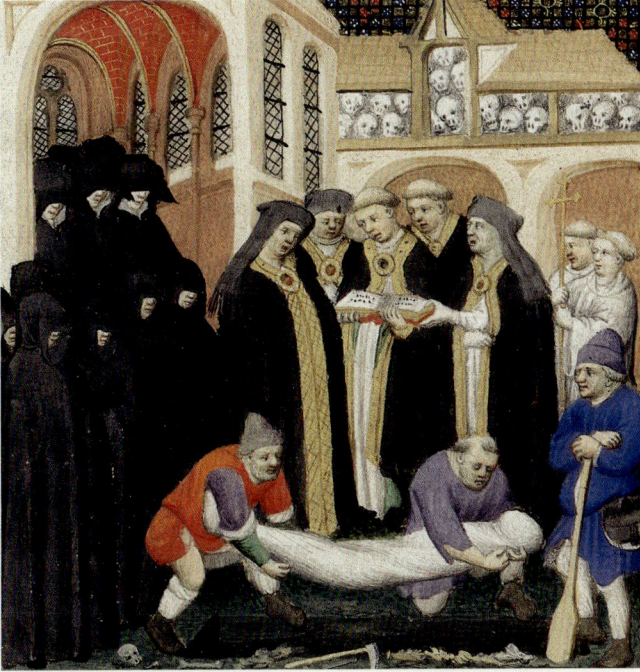

Left: *Overcrowding in the abbey cemeteries meant that many graves were dug over by the later Middle Ages. The disinterred bones were kept in a charnel house, as shown in the background of this illustration in a French manuscript of about 1410 showing the burial of the dead*

Below: *Graves excavated at the base of Ethelbert's Tower in the early 20th century*

Burials at St Augustine's

By the end of the Middle Ages the abbey church, cloister and chapter house contained hundreds of graves, including those of kings, queens and archbishops.

For reasons relating to spiritual salvation, medieval Christians took place of burial extremely seriously. The most desirable locations were monasteries, where most people were buried in earth graves in an outdoor cemetery. The monks had a separate outdoor cemetery restricted for their use. Before the Norman Conquest the privilege of burial inside a church was restricted to founders, rulers, bishops and abbots, but with time it extended to virtually anyone able to afford a generous gift to the church.

At St Augustine's the most prestigious graves were always those of the Anglo-Saxon kings and archbishops, concentrated in the churches of SS Peter and Paul and of St Mary. But there were other important graves, not least that of St Mildred (see page 31). St Mary's also contained tombs, including those of four kings of Kent together with their queens and their children. Altogether, the monks had custody of the graves of eleven archbishops, seven kings and their queens, and various other dignitaries. With time, many of these individuals were recognized as saints and their holy remains moved (or 'translated') to gilded shrines within the post-Conquest church.

Above: The north wall of the church nave from the south. The clustered shafts defined the three-storey bays and corresponded to the main piers of the nave, the remains of which can be seen in the foreground

Below: Part of the decorative frieze that adorned the belfry stage of Ethelbert's Tower by the time the Norman rebuilding was finished in the early 12th century

Scolland's decision to build from the east was conventional, and allowed the monks to continue to use the Anglo-Saxon Church of SS Peter and Paul until a new presbytery was available, whereupon the old church could be demolished to make way for the transept and nave. By Scolland's death in 1087 work had progressed at least as far as the transept. The piers for the great central tower, positioned above the site of Wulfric's ill-fated rotunda, must also have been rising by then.

Concluding Work

The next abbot, Wido (r.1087–93), is credited in historical sources with most of the remaining work, including the central tower itself, the transept and the nave. It is likely it was finished under his successor, Hugh de Flori (r.1099–1126), however, as completion by 1093 seems improbable for such elaborate, costly and logistically complex work. When finished, the monks had an architecturally unified church almost 110m long.

Western Towers

When lay people were permitted access to the church it may have been through the west door. The visitor passed between the two massively built towers, traditionally named after St Augustine and St Ethelbert (as the converted pagan king came to be known). Each was copiously banded and arcaded with carved decoration, and finished off with polygonal turrets. Ethelbert's Tower, to the north, stood largely intact until 1822. The thickness of its inner wall can still be appreciated.

Nave

The nave stretched east in a series of 11 equal bays defined by the main piers. Flanking it were lower, stone-vaulted aisles, with galleries above them. The whole was well lit by windows at aisle, gallery and clerestory level. The high central space seems always to have had a wooden ceiling rather than a stone vault. On the north side, where the wall survives to its highest level, the arrangement can best be appreciated. The bays rise in three storeys, with the blocked aisle windows at second-storey level and the smaller gallery windows at the third. The clustered shafts that define the bays supported the aisle vaults, which sprang from the cushion capitals above the shafts. The vaults were supported on the other side of the aisle by identical shafts attached to the outer faces of the main piers. The brick patchwork here postdates the abbey's suppression.

Choir and the Crossing

The monks' choir with its wooden stalls and reading desks occupied the three eastern bays of the nave and the crossing space under the central tower. It was divided from the rest of the nave by two high transverse screens: the rood screen, which was topped by a great crucifix and stood roughly on the site of the main Anglo-Saxon church, and a more substantial screen called a pulpitum. The lay visitor would have been permitted past these screens only on special occasions such as the feast days of the saints to whom the chapels were dedicated, and then only via the aisles leading into the north and south transepts, rather than directly through the choir.

The crossing was defined by four great piers, the surviving rubble cores of which indicate the bulk needed to support the tower. Much of the crossing's original area is now occupied by the excavated crypt of Wulfric's rotunda. The north and south transepts extended either side of the crossing, each with an apsidal chapel projecting from its east wall; that to the north was dedicated to St John the Evangelist, that to the south to St John the Baptist. The remains of some of the Kentish kings were relocated from the Anglo-Saxon churches to the south transept and presumably furnished with new monuments.

Above: An unusually fine example of a pilgrim badge from St Augustine's showing Christ in a bejewelled tunic. Such badges were distributed at pilgrimage sites and were believed to bestow on the wearer the benefits of the relics visited

Below: An engraving by William Stukeley of Ethelbert's Tower in 1722 from the north-west. The south tower would have been similar. To the left are the remains of the abbot's chapel

The New Presbytery

In 1414 a monk of the abbey, Thomas of Elmham, made a drawing of the church presbytery, recording fascinating details of the church interior.

A remarkable pen-and-ink drawing in a manuscript made in 1414 at St Augustine's Abbey presents a view into the abbey presbytery. By this time the Norman building had been remodelled with larger windows and carved work in an early Gothic style, but the main lines of the Norman arrangement are still clear.

The drawing's perspective is deliberately inaccurate to direct the viewer's attention and thus potentially confusing to a modern viewer. The high altar is at the bottom, with a 14th-century screen behind it and flanking doors labelled 'to the bodies of the saints'.

Mounted on the screen is the shrine of Ethelbert, the founding king now raised to saintly status, together with (higher up) two reliquaries of St Liudhard (Queen Bertha's chaplain) and six books, identified as 'the books sent by Gregory to Augustine'. There are also images of the risen Christ and two cherubim. Around the presbytery walls and in its three apsidal chapels stand 13 house-shaped shrines containing relics of the archbishops, St Mildred and Abbot Hadrian (r.669–710).

It is clear how the ambulatory allowed pilgrims to pass from one shrine to the next in orderly fashion. St Augustine's shrine has the position of honour in the chapel of the Holy Trinity at the top of the drawing.

Above: This figure of a saint from the abbey once adorned a reliquary, perhaps one of the many housed in the presbytery. It was made in Limoges in the 13th century of copper with mercury gilding, enamel and eyes of blue glass

Right: A carved support in the chapel of St Thomas in the crypt; the three crypt chapels mirrored those of the presbytery above

Facing page: Thomas of Elmham's drawing of the new presbytery, included in his history of the abbey

Facing page, bottom: The south-east chapel in the crypt, dedicated to St Thomas the Apostle. Medieval tiles remain on the floor and the niche on the left is likely to have contained a piscina, the basin in which the priest washed his hands after Mass

Presbytery and Crypt

Beyond the crossing stood the presbytery, the most sacred part of the church, where the high altar was situated. It seems to have been slightly elevated, and so accessed by a short flight of steps. As in many Norman churches the presbytery ended in an apse. The central space, which had a wooden ceiling rather than a vault, was surrounded by a vaulted ambulatory for the use of visitors to the chapels and shrines. Projecting from the curved eastern wall were three apsidal chapels. The central chapel at the east end, immediately behind the high altar, was dedicated to the Holy Trinity, that to the north-east to the Holy Innocents, and that to the south-east to the

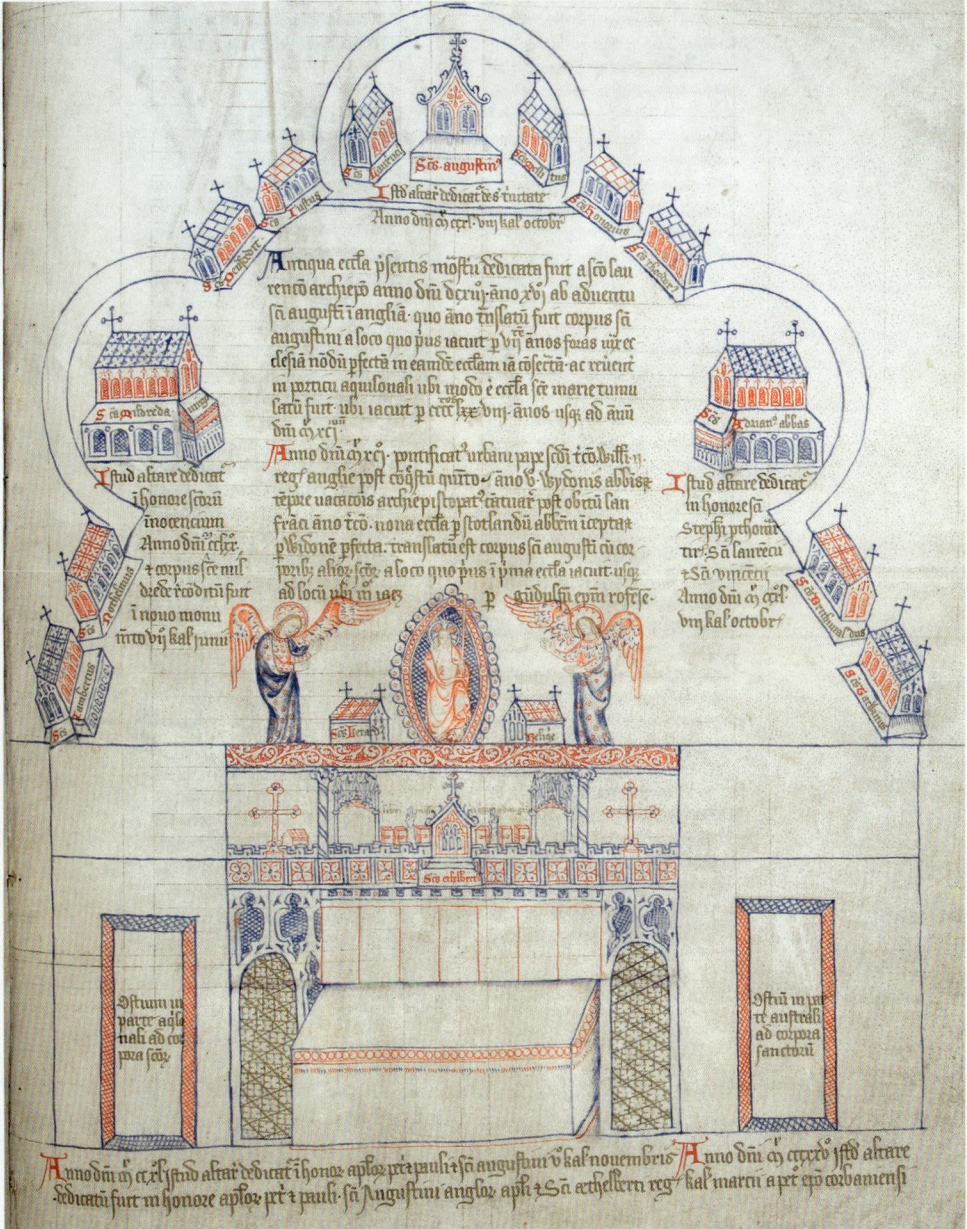

sainted deacons Stephen, Laurence and Vincent. Below the presbytery was a spacious crypt. Its floor plan mirrored that of the presbytery, with three apsidal chapels with their own dedications directly below those of the presbytery.

The central chapel, following a widespread English custom of the dedication of the most easterly chapel within a church, was dedicated to the Virgin Mary. A modern replica altar has been set up where the original altar stood. Behind this was a large image of the Virgin, renewed in 1325. The crypt was accessible to monks and pilgrims via steps from both the north and south transepts. It is now open to view, the entire presbytery having been demolished.

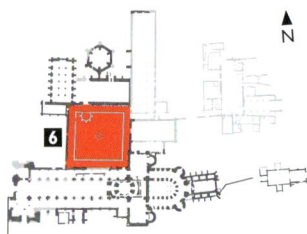

Above: Part of an enamelled plaque with a depiction – rare for the time – of a centaur using a bow and arrow; 13th century, perhaps originally from Limoges

Below: The cloister of the former Dominican convent in Colmar, France, which was built in 1283. The cloister at St Augustine's, as built in about 1276, had a similar arrangement: a stone arcade with elaborate tracery supported on a low wall, and a timber, rather than a vaulted, ceiling

6 CLOISTER

The enclosed space that formed the cloister had a special significance for medieval monks as both a microcosm of their monastery and a symbol of their secluded life. Opportunities to reflect on this symbolism were built into monastic routine. Each morning during the later Middle Ages, for example, the brethren sat silently in the eastern alley, or walk, of their cloister with their abbot and prior, who had dedicated seats flanking the chapter-house door.

The cloister also had practical purposes. Primarily, it permitted easy circulation between the abbey's main buildings, all of which communicated with it via passages or stairways, but its four covered alleys served various other functions too, making it a more flexible space than most others in the abbey. Cloisters were usually built on the sunnier, south side of a monastery. At St Augustine's, however, the cloister was built to the north, as there was insufficient room to the south for the extended complex of buildings that depended on the cloister.

Changes to the Abbey Cloister

The Anglo-Saxon cloister, the foundations of which have been excavated, was considerably smaller than the one seen today, in line with the smaller size of the pre-Conquest church. This early cloister was probably rebuilt in the tenth century. During the Norman works a new cloister was laid out under Abbot Scolland and completed in the early 12th century. The remains of the cloister seen today are the result of a further rebuilding, in about 1276, which preserved the Norman dimensions. It is comparatively large, with alleys about 40m long – roughly the same size as the cloister at the cathedral. While the alleys of the latter were vaulted in stone, those at St Augustine's had timber ceilings and roofs, with lead or tiles for weatherproofing.

Left: St Dunstan, who led a reform of English monasticism in the tenth century, is shown here as an archbishop writing a commentary to the Rule of St Benedict; illuminated page of a manuscript created at the cathedral priory at Canterbury, 1170–80

Below: A Corinthian capital, dating from the seventh to the ninth centuries, probably from the Church of SS Peter and Paul

The Monastic Life

St Augustine's Abbey belonged to the Benedictine order, the only monastic order existing in England before the Norman Conquest.

The monks of St Augustine's observed the Rule for monastic conduct written by St Benedict of Nursia (d.c.547). Although Augustine and his fellow missionaries may not have followed the Benedictine Rule themselves, it was probably adopted early in the abbey's history and was presumably reaffirmed when St Dunstan (d.988), as Archbishop of Canterbury, led a reform of English monasticism.

In 73 short chapters, the Rule presents both a handbook for establishing a monastery and a guide to how monks should live. While the principal theme is how to celebrate divine service, other topics include the ranks of monk and servant required by a monastery, communal living, the abbot's authority and responsibilities, correction of bad behaviour, and provision of food and drink. Ownership of private property by individual monks is presented as a serious crime. A short document written in Italy in the sixth century was naturally inadequate to the requirements of a large English abbey, and there is evidence that the monks formally asked the pope to recognize certain mitigations of the Rule in the 1270s. Nevertheless, the abbey's customary – a more detailed book of regulations written specifically for use at St Augustine's – also directs that the Rule should be respected and read aloud on various formal occasions.

Above: Three bosses, carved to represent the heads of lions and that (centre) of a green man. They decorated the intersecting ribs of the vaulted ceiling of the chapter house as rebuilt in the 1320s and 1330s

Below right: A photograph looking north along the east alley of the cloister while it was under excavation in the early 20th century. The remains of the alley paving can clearly be seen

Below: This bench end was built into the south side of the monks' parlour off the east cloister alley. It probably dates from the final stage of Norman rebuilding under Abbot Hugh de Flori in the early 12th century

The alleys were paved with plain, square tiles and tombstones. Arcades supporting the alley roofs along each side of the cloister formed bays containing large windows on a raised stone base. The position of this base is now marked by a plinth surrounding the garth (central cloister space). There is no evidence that the windows, which contained elaborate stone tracery, were glazed (although glazed cloisters were later built at Benedictine abbeys such as Gloucester and Peterborough).

East Alley

In the middle of the east alley is the sill of a wide doorway that led into a large, oblong building called a chapter house, after the practice of reading a chapter of St Benedict's Rule at the beginning of the meetings held here every morning. Here the monks discussed business, commemorated their dead and addressed any misdemeanours committed by individual monks.

The Norman chapter house was renovated in the 1320s and 1330s, when highly decorative Gothic stalls were inserted. Although nothing of this work remains *in situ*, many exquisitely carved fragments of the stalls' canopies, bearing traces of blue, red and gold paint, have been excavated. The monks sat around the periphery of the room in their canopied stalls with

the abbot enthroned at the centre of the east wall. (The cathedral chapter house, also rebuilt in the late Middle Ages, gives some idea of these arrangements, and their splendour.)

Between the chapter house and the church was a narrower building not accessible from the cloister. It appears to have been a treasury where valuables such as relics and reliquaries, vestments, money and liturgical books were stored. A room above it lined with cupboards may have been a document or book store. A library is attested in 1340, when it is called a 'bochouse', but its exact location is unknown.

South Alley

At the east end of the south alley are traces of another grand doorway. This was the processional entrance to the monks' choir and, on the evidence of other such doorways, must have been richly sculpted. Beside it was a wall recess, probably a book cupboard. Monks did much of their reading in the cloister and copies of standard books of monastic education were kept here even after the library was built. West of this doorway, along the wall, stood a row of desks where individual monks could study (such study space existed in the cloisters of many abbeys; examples can still be seen at Gloucester Cathedral).

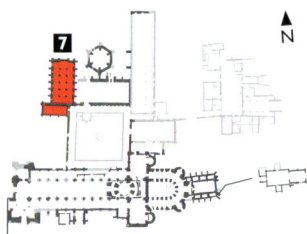

Above right: A sketch of 1785 by John Carter from the site of the abbot's lodgings looking south to the remains of his chapel. The north wall of the chapel is still standing. To the left of the wall stub towards its east end are its ground- and first-floor doorways, granting access from the abbot's lodgings. That at ground level led into a vaulted chamber and out onto the west alley

Below: One of the apertures, perhaps a window, in the west alley

West Alley

The west alley ran parallel to the abbot's lodgings. The abbot's private apartments were at first-floor level, while the rooms on the ground floor (colder and damper in winter) had more commonplace uses. These buildings, later incorporated into the post-Suppression palace, have now vanished, but indications of them are visible in the surviving wall, which contains three doorways and some windows.

The doorway at the south end of the alley was once elaborately embellished and led into a vaulted room, above which was the abbot's private chapel. The chapel was accessible both from a stair below and at first-floor level from the abbot's apartments. At the centre of the alley a door led to chambers probably used by the abbot's personal servants. At the north end, a doorway (now giving access to the library of St Augustine's College) led to the undercroft of the abbot's great chamber.

North Alley

The monks' refectory, where they ate, was entered from the north alley. This long, rectangular hall stood on a low undercroft. Three of the steps that led up to it remain at the west end of the alley. At the east end of the refectory was a raised dais where the abbot's table stood and above which was a wall-painting of Christ in Majesty. There was also an elevated pulpit, from which a monk read passages from Bible commentaries while the others ate.

In the cloister garth, opposite the refectory door, stood a seven-sided water tower above a lavatorium, or washbasin, for ritual and casual ablutions. Water was brought into the cloister from a conduit house to the north-east of the abbey precinct via stone channels and lead pipes (sections of these pipes have been found). The inner wall of the north alley also contains traces of at least nine cupboards in the form of blocked-up, round-headed arches with sills set above pavement level. These may also have been used for storing books.

☑ ABBOT'S HALL

As the figurehead of a rich and ancient monastery, the abbot of St Augustine's was expected to flaunt his status. He was obliged to entertain lavishly and to dispense significant charity: to meet these obligations, he received a large share of the monastery's annual income. Grand buildings were the most effective means of ostentation and no part of the abbot's lodgings was more impressive than the hall: a rectangular building aligned on a north–south axis with an internal length of about 24m. Its outline (but no detail) is preserved in the 19th-century library of St Augustine's College, which stands on its foundations. The hall space, at first-floor level, was flooded with light by large windows and heraldry probably featured significantly in its decoration. As a site of ceremony as well as entertainment, it was no doubt intimidating as well as marvellous, depending on the visitor's status.

Above: The north alley of the cloister. Beyond it, to the right, is the site of the monks' refectory, at the far end of which is the library of St Augustine's College. One of the cupboards in the north alley can be seen on the right

Below: A tinted lithograph by Louis Razé, 1847, of the quadrangle of St Augustine's College, looking towards the library, which stands on the site of the abbot's hall

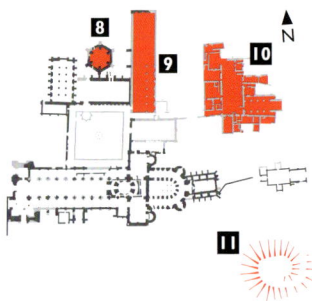

A Norman church
B Abbot's hall and lodgings
C Refectory
D Kitchen
E Dormitory
F Infirmary complex
G Church of St Pancras
H Campanile
I Outer precinct

8 KITCHEN

There were two large kitchens at St Augustine's, one for the monks, the other for the abbot. The monastic kitchen, rebuilt in the late 13th century, lay north of the refectory, to which it was joined by service rooms (buttery, pantry and larder). It was hexagonal in plan, some 13m across, and presumably had large fireplaces in at least four of its angles, for an observer in the 17th century counted eight chimneys. Drainage channels for fat and water were set in and underneath the pavement.

9 DORMITORY

The monks' dormitory was a large, rectangular room more than 60m long, on the north side of the chapter house and running at right angles to it. It was first constructed during the Norman rebuilding and then renovated in the 13th century. The two isolated buttresses visible today standing next to the site of the monastic kitchen belonged to it.

The dormitory was raised on an undercroft, with a stair at its south end descending to the east alley of the cloister. On its east side was an aisle, whose piers may have marked out the cells of senior monks. Most of the monks, however, had beds arranged along the lateral walls. By the 13th century it was common monastic practice for the spaces around monks' beds to be segregated and thus 'personalized' by curtains, and this custom was probably followed at St Augustine's. The monastic reredorter, a vast latrine as long as the dormitory itself, adjoined the north end of the dormitory.

10 INFIRMARY

The infirmary complex, which was begun soon after 1066 but later considerably altered, lay to the north of St Pancras's Church and east of the dormitory. It was reached from the cloister's east alley through a passage running under the dormitory. The principal buildings of the infirmary were a large hall, which contained beds for sick and aged monks, as well as those recovering from bleeding (a regular procedure for all monks, thought to prevent disease), and a chapel. Two sculpted figures (now in the visitor centre) probably come from this chapel's reredos, a decorative screen installed behind the altar as a solemn backdrop to celebration of the Mass.

One of these figures, shown in archiepiscopal vestments, probably represented St Augustine. Hall and chapel were surrounded by subsidiary buildings, which included private chambers for retired senior monks and important laypeople.

11 CAMPANILE MOUND AND LAY CEMETERY

Most of the abbey's ancillary buildings were located north of the central axis of the church. The exceptions were the Cemetery Gate and a bell tower, or campanile, isolated on a man-made knoll in the south-east of the precinct. The campanile was associated with a lay cemetery that occupied most of the south side of the site between the church and the precinct wall running beside the Longport. The monks had a separate cemetery on the south side of the infirmary.

The main peal of bells was located in the church and the campanile, which was evidently rather small, presumably existed for the tolling of funerals. Despite the large available area, there was considerable digging over of earlier graves to accommodate later ones and in the late Middle Ages there was a charnel house, for disinterred bones, which is recorded to have displayed an image of the Virgin Mary.

All the buildings mentioned above occupied the inner part of the abbey. Beyond this area, to the east and north of the monastic complex, there was an outer precinct occupied by vineyards and gardens. The monks also had a home (or 'demesne') farm, situated outside the precincts to the south, which supplied much of their food.

Above: A 14th-century statue of an abbot in Mass vestments, probably representing St Augustine himself. It was excavated on the site of the infirmary chapel

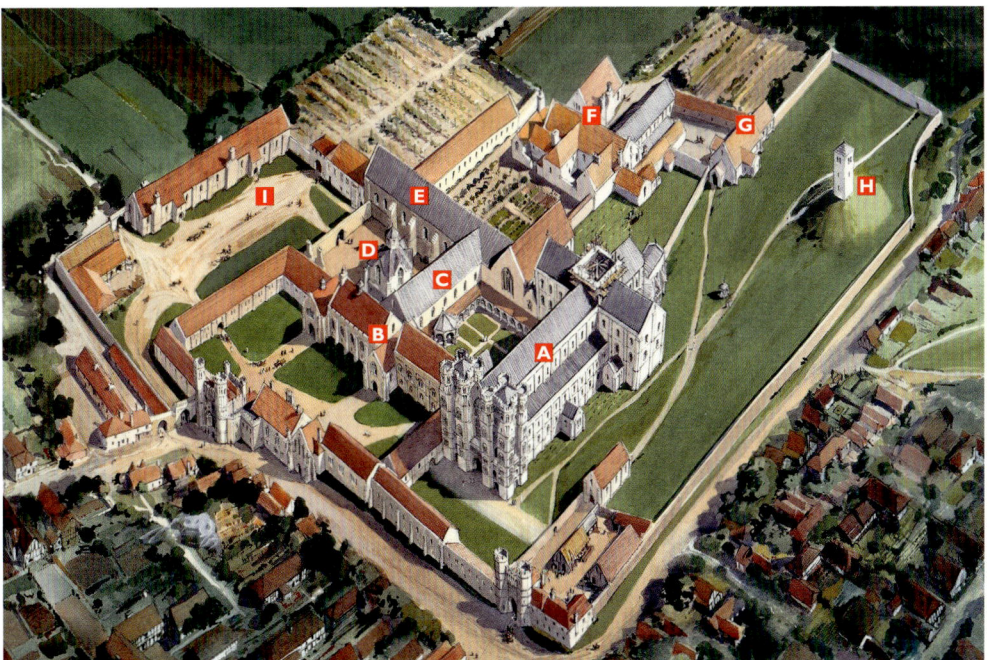

ASICLA DO[] LUCAS TENETUR

History of the Abbey

ARRIVAL OF ST AUGUSTINE

In AD 596 Pope Gregory I sent a mission from Rome with the intention of spreading Christianity throughout England. This was the mission of St Augustine. At this time the Christianity that had flourished in much of Britain under Roman rule was effectively extinct. The existing Christian communities, confined to Wales, Scotland and some peripheral parts of England, owed their existence to Irish missionaries and so identified as 'Celtic' rather than 'Roman'.

Augustine and his party of missionary monks travelled from Rome through the Frankish kingdoms of Gaul and must have crossed the Channel at or near Boulogne as, in the spring of 597, they landed in the Isle of Thanet in north-east Kent. Gregory had envisaged that Augustine would settle in London. King Ethelbert of Kent, however, offered Augustine some open ground to the east of Canterbury for a monastery and another site within the walls for a cathedral. This was evidently decisive and the monks established themselves in what the Venerable Bede (d.735) in his *Ecclesiastical History of the English People* calls the Kentish 'metropolis'. Canterbury had been a Roman city of some size and had a church whose foundations would later be used for the cathedral.

THE FIRST ABBEY

It is probably no coincidence that the abbey site was close to both a Roman cemetery and the pre-existing Church of St Martin, used by the Christian Queen Bertha, wife of King Ethelbert, and her chaplain Liudhard. The missionaries could use St Martin's to worship and perform their pastoral work of preaching and baptism while their abbey was built. The work was financed by Ethelbert, for Augustine's mission would not have risked travelling with significant funds.

Bede mentions Ethelbert's role as builder of the Church of SS Peter and Paul, but the king presumably also funded the early monastic buildings, including a dormitory, refectory of sorts and perhaps a primitive cloister. The monks themselves must have decided the form and layout of the abbey buildings with reference to what they knew of Roman and Frankish examples. While the church was built of brick and cement, these ancillary buildings were made largely or wholly of timber and had to be big enough for about 40 monks, a number that grew over time. Ethelbert began the work of endowing the monastery with lands, through which process it became financially independent.

Above: An ivory comb, decorated with animals and foliage, which bears an inscription on its side declaring it was sent by Pope Gregory the Great to Queen Bertha. In fact it dates from the 12th century, but its survival indicates the great importance placed on this early event

Below: Detail of a 14th-century English manuscript showing King Ethelbert of Kent inside a font being baptized by St Augustine

Facing page: The opening page of the gospel of St Luke from a sixth-century copy of the gospels thought to have been given by Pope Gregory to Augustine to take with him on his mission. As such it was revered, and displayed with a number of other valued manuscripts above the high altar of the abbey church

Manuscripts at the Abbey

The abbey had one of the largest book collections of any English monastery, only a fraction of which survives.

Above: *The opening of Psalm 27, showing King David with his musicians, from the 'Vespasian Psalter'. It dates in part from the eighth century and, according to Thomas Elmham, one of the monks of St Augustine's, stood on the high altar of the abbey church*

Below: *An oyster shell found at the abbey. It contains traces of blue pigment, made from azurite, which would have been used to illuminate manuscripts*

With the possible exception of Canterbury Cathedral Priory, St Augustine's in the late Middle Ages had the largest known library of any English monastery: some 1,900 volumes are listed in the surviving catalogue, of which about 300 survive.

The acquisition of books began with the foundation of the abbey, for books were needed by monks for a range of practical and symbolic purposes. Augustine brought Italian books to England which were given to him by Pope Gregory. Over time these early books became relics and were displayed above the high altar; Thomas of Elmham called them 'the first fruits of our religious life'. (A copy of the gospels kept at Corpus Christi College, Cambridge, and used today at the installation of archbishops of Canterbury is thought to be one of these; see page 26.)

Books for everyday use were produced steadily by the Anglo-Saxon monks. They used the skin of sheep (parchment) or calves (vellum), upon which they ruled lines for writing on, using lead or a purpose-made knife for scoring. When making books as gifts or status symbols, they often added images in paint and gold. The so-called Vespasian Psalter, made in about 725–50, possibly at the abbey, is a vivid example of the collaboration of artists and scribes to produce books of great beauty.

An early impetus for book creation was the so-called Canterbury School, started by Abbot Hadrian (r.669–710) and Theodore, Archbishop of Canterbury. The school introduced Anglo-Saxon scholars to new, Continental learning in law, philosophy, biblical interpretation, medicine and rhetoric, and books were the cornerstone of this learning.

Theological and legal scholarship was fostered throughout the abbey's life. Its library was divided into two sections, one housing books on theology, the other on everything else. Among these other works were titles on canon and civil law, philosophy (largely commentaries on works by Aristotle), history, nature, letter collections, grammar, poetry, geometry, astronomy and medicine.

During his rule as abbot, Thomas Findon (r.1283–1310) greatly expanded the library and in the later Middle Ages student monks took books to and from the abbey and the University of Oxford. A notable manuscript of the mid 14th century, a learned work of natural philosophy, was brought to St Augustine's from Oxford, where it had probably been made. Near the beginning is a drawing of John the Baptist, a saint identified as a proto-monk because of his solitary habits. It reminded monks temporarily living outside the cloister at Oxford of the core values of their religious vocation.

By this time, relatively few manuscripts were made by monks. Book production had become a commercial, secular activity and the monastery bought much from the book trade, which was centred in London. Some monks went on making books of miscellaneous content for personal use, however. One such monk, Clement of Canterbury (d.c.1500), was a dedicated annotator of the abbey's books. He left notes and drawings in dozens of the surviving volumes. The attitude to such activity was evidently different at St Augustine's from what it is in modern libraries.

Below: A stylus, used to guide the pen as the scribe wrote, and a bone-handled 'pricker', for piercing a sheet of parchment to mark lines on a sheet beneath

Bottom: Illustration of John the Baptist from a manuscript produced in Oxford, 1330–40. It belonged to John of Lingfield, a monk of St Augustine's and later a lecturer on canon law at Oxford

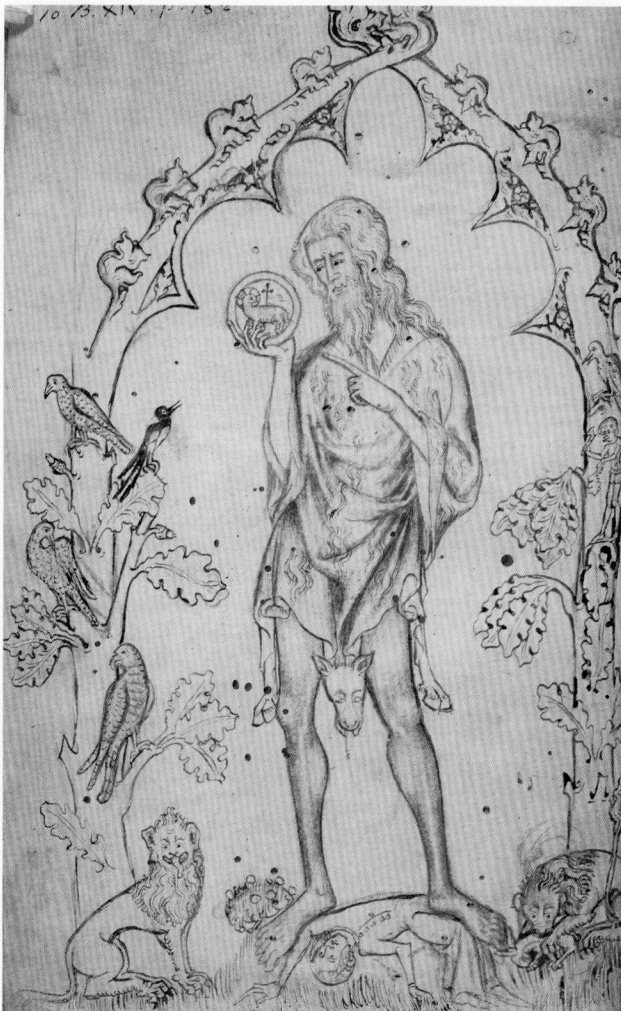

Above: Detail of a psalter made, probably for Dunstan at Canterbury, at the end of the tenth century. It includes the Office according to the Rule of St Benedict, the only monastic rule in use in England at the time

Right: Anglo-Saxon builders shown at work on a tower from a manuscript of the Hexateuch (the first six books of the Bible) that belonged to St Augustine's Abbey and was created in Canterbury; c.1025–1150

Below: Section of a cross shaft from the Church of SS Peter and Paul, late 10th or early 11th century. It was probably part of building works related to Dunstan's reforms

REFORMS AND WORKS UNDER DUNSTAN

Little is recorded of the history of St Augustine's between the eighth and the tenth centuries. The period was one of sporadic growth, during which the monks acquired property and privileges but also witnessed setbacks, including, in the mid eighth century, the abbey's loss of status as burial place of the archbishops, who were instead buried in their cathedral.

It is not certain that the abbey was continuously occupied by monks during the Anglo-Saxon period, although scholars generally assume that it was. During the ninth and early tenth centuries English monasticism suffered much destruction and neglect, not least due to Viking activity. From the mid tenth century attempts were made to invigorate and unify monastic observance through the promotion of the Benedictine Rule, the most influential of all medieval guides to monastic life, written in the sixth century. The most significant reformers were Aethelwold (d.984), Abbot of Abingdon and later Bishop of Winchester, and Dunstan (d.988), Abbot of Glastonbury and, from 960, Archbishop of Canterbury.

Dunstan evidently admired St Augustine's and revered its founder. His rededication of what was then still the separate Church of SS Peter and Paul in 978, adding the name of Augustine to the two apostles, may well relate to reform at the abbey, although the Benedictine Rule was probably already

in use here. But no effort of internal reform could deflect external aggression and Abbot Aelfmaer (r.1006–c.1027) was captured and held hostage when the Vikings raided Canterbury in 1011 (killing Archbishop Alphege in the process). When the Danish king Cnut conquered and was crowned king of England in 1016, however, he granted privileges to St Augustine's. One such privilege was permission to translate the relics of Mildred (d.c.734), the first abbess of the nunnery at Minster-in-Thanet, which had become defunct, to the abbey church, where she was venerated alongside the early archbishops.

NORMAN REBUILDING

The Norman Conquest had a powerful effect on the politics of the English Church as well as its architecture. St Augustine's was caught up in this, and although it kept most of its endowments, its last Anglo-Saxon abbot, Aethelsige, was forced to resign in 1070 in favour of the Norman monk Scolland. The next two abbots, Wido and Hugh de Flori, were also Frenchmen: both were roundly hated by the monks and Wido's appointment was violently resisted.

Only in 1126 was another English-born abbot, Hugh of Trottiscliffe (r.1126–51), installed (the rank-and-file monks, however, remained predominantly English throughout the Norman period). By Trottiscliffe's time, the abbey church and associated complex had been transformed from a venerable but architecturally modest collection of buildings into one of the most impressive monasteries in northern Europe.

Abbot Scolland's Works

Scolland (r.1070–87) was not indifferent to St Augustine's status as England's oldest monastery. Like Norman abbots elsewhere in England, he came to identify with local traditions. Respect for sanctity transcended patriotism and Scolland's rebuilding, and the work done by his followers, should be seen in this light. The new buildings, although modelled on Norman architecture, honoured the mother church of the English by their size and grandeur. They also housed a larger community: 61 monks are recorded at the abbey in 1146 and the choir, chapter house, dormitory and refectory had capacity for many more. Although these buildings were altered in the 13th and 14th centuries, they retained their Norman dimensions until the Suppression. They were clearly capable of accommodating the 84 monks recorded in 1423.

When considering the size of Norman monastic buildings, at St Augustine's and elsewhere, it is important to remember that the abbots who commissioned them were not only providing for the monks they ruled: they expected and planned for the growth of their monastic communities. Such grand buildings may even have been intended to encourage this growth, thereby contributing to the country's spiritual health

Above: A seax, a typical Saxon combat knife (after which the Saxons were named) found at the abbey. The monks' lives were not entirely peaceful – a Viking raid in 1011 led to the capture of their abbot and the murder of the archbishop

Below: A voussoir (wedge-shaped stone) from an arch at the east end of the church, with striking remnants of red and black paint on a white ground. It probably dates from the Norman rebuilding

(which could be estimated to an extent by numbers of monks).
The enlarged presbytery of the Norman church also increased
the abbey's capacity to accommodate pilgrimage. Little
information survives about pilgrimage to the tombs of the early
archbishops, and it is assumed that most pilgrims had not
travelled far. What is certain is that after 1170 the relics at
St Augustine's were eclipsed in popular imagination by the cult
of St Thomas Becket at the cathedral.

Scolland's work in the late 11th century on the new
presbytery, with its ambulatory and apsidal chapels, was clearly
designed to allow for the circulation of a large number of
visitors, who could progress up one side of the nave and exit
down the other. Whatever the volume of pilgrimage traffic at
the time, Scolland and his advisors probably took the long view
in their work to glorify the abbey's saints, planning for an
increase in pilgrim numbers. He could not have anticipated the
future dominance of Becket's cult.

Above: A detail from a parchment
roll showing abbots in the
procession of Parliament in 1512;
the abbot of St Augustine's was
one of the heads of religious
houses traditionally summoned.
He is shown towards the right
beneath the abbey arms of a white
cross on a black ground, flanked by
the abbots of Bury St Edmunds
and St Albans

Abbots of St Augustine's

*As head of the first monastery in England, the abbot of
St Augustine's had a special status in the Church.*

St Augustine's had about 70
abbots from its foundation to
its Suppression. These men
were always subordinate in
ecclesiastical matters to the
archbishops of Canterbury,
whose seat was the cathedral,
itself part of another monastery
from about 997 within the city
walls. St Augustine's, however,
considered itself especially
privileged in relation to both
the cathedral and the English
Church in general. Thomas of

THE LATE MEDIEVAL ABBEY

The history of St Augustine's from the 13th century until the Suppression is well documented. Several chronicles survive, the most important by William Thorne, a monk of St Augustine's. Thorne, writing in the 1390s, was deeply concerned about the dignity of his abbey. His chronicle is largely a partisan account of its extended struggle to protect its ancient rights, particularly the contested one of exemption from archiepiscopal interference. The main villains of the piece are various archbishops of Canterbury, occasionally abetted by the papacy.

Since the late 11th century, the archbishops had asserted rights of jurisdiction in relation to St Augustine's which the monks considered to violate their abbey's vaunted status as the wellspring of English Christianity. Monastic resistance to this – in the law courts, and occasionally through shows of physical force – was a constant element of the abbey's late medieval history, and helps to explain why the Great Gate and

Above: An earthenware sundial found at the abbey. It dates from the 14th or early 15th century

Elmham, a monk at the abbey, put the matter thus: 'anyone of sane mind must see that ours was the first community of monks established in England; the monastery was founded from no other monastery established earlier elsewhere in England, but all others derived from it'.

On this basis, the abbot of St Augustine's claimed to be the moral, the historical and in some respects the legal equal of the archbishop, a circumstance which caused chronic tensions, particularly in relation to the archbishop's rights to visit the abbey and correct its faults. From the Norman Conquest right up until the Suppression, the abbots had much to do to defend the abbey's rights. They also had to defend its property against both secular and ecclesiastical litigants: litigation, particularly in relation to real estate and revenue-generating privileges, was a constant

problem for all large monasteries during this period. The abbey's chronicles present St Augustine's as an embattled but proud institution led by heroic abbots. The later abbots of St Augustine's rivalled bishops in their display. They had magnificent lodgings and possessed the right to wear a mitre and other pontifical ornaments (granted by the pope in 1179), a privilege which the heads of many large monasteries were to obtain. As great landed aristocrats, they also had a seat in Parliament among the Lords Spiritual.

Above: The tomb of Abbot Roger II (r.1252–72) as found in the south transept of the abbey church during excavations in 1918
Left: The lead chalice buried with Abbot Dunster (r.1482–96). It was usual for burials to contain base metal imitations of the precious objects the abbots would have used in life

Cemetery Gate look so martial. Simultaneously, religious culture continued to flourish at St Augustine's. A large rectangular Lady chapel was built to the east of their presbytery between 1496 and 1510, and some time about 1530 the monks contracted the printer John Mychell (d.1556) to publish an account of some of St Augustine's miracles. Mychell's press was apparently set up within the monastery.

THE SUPPRESSION
The suppression of the monasteries under King Henry VIII (r.1509–47) began in earnest in 1536. Its main purpose was to appropriate the vast amounts of land in religious hands in order to increase Crown revenues. St Augustine's was dissolved on 30 July 1538. At that time, it realized an annual income from its

lands in Kent, Surrey, London and elsewhere of about £1,400, making it the 14th or 15th richest monastery in England. There is no detailed record of the events of 30 July, but the letter of surrender survives, bearing the signatures of Abbot John Essex and 30 other monks. It is a tragic document in the light of what it signed away, but the monks dared not resist, knowing of the brutal way that Henry VIII dealt with monastic defiance.

Each of the monks received a life pension. As usual, the abbot got the largest sum, as well as possession for life of the nearby (and very lucrative) manor of Sturry. The core monastic buildings were rapidly demolished, although some structures were retained and converted into wings of a royal palace. Large quantities of precious objects, including gilded silver images of St Augustine and St Ethelbert and a reliquary containing part of Ethelbert's skull, were taken to the royal treasury in the Tower of London. The main shrines of Augustine and the other saints were probably broken up on site and the relics thrown away or destroyed. Mercifully, many of the abbey's manuscripts seem to have remained somewhere on site until after 1550, when book collectors who cared about their preservation obtained them.

A ROYAL PALACE

The abbot's apartments were coveted by Henry VIII, who had stayed in them more than once before the Suppression. In autumn 1539 the process of converting them into a royal palace began, with the aim of completing the work by December, when Anne of Cleves, the fourth of Henry's wives, was due to stay overnight in Canterbury on her way from Deal to London. Anne only stayed one night, but the renovation continued for over a decade.

Above: A fragment from one of the canopies above the monks' stalls in the chapter house, as rebuilt in the early 14th century. This piece depicts a man grimacing in pain as a hand grabs his hair

Below: A view of the abbey site taken from the tower of Canterbury Cathedral in about 1655 by Thomas Johnson. Ethelbert's Tower is still standing, as is the abbot's hall and a range of buildings connected to it

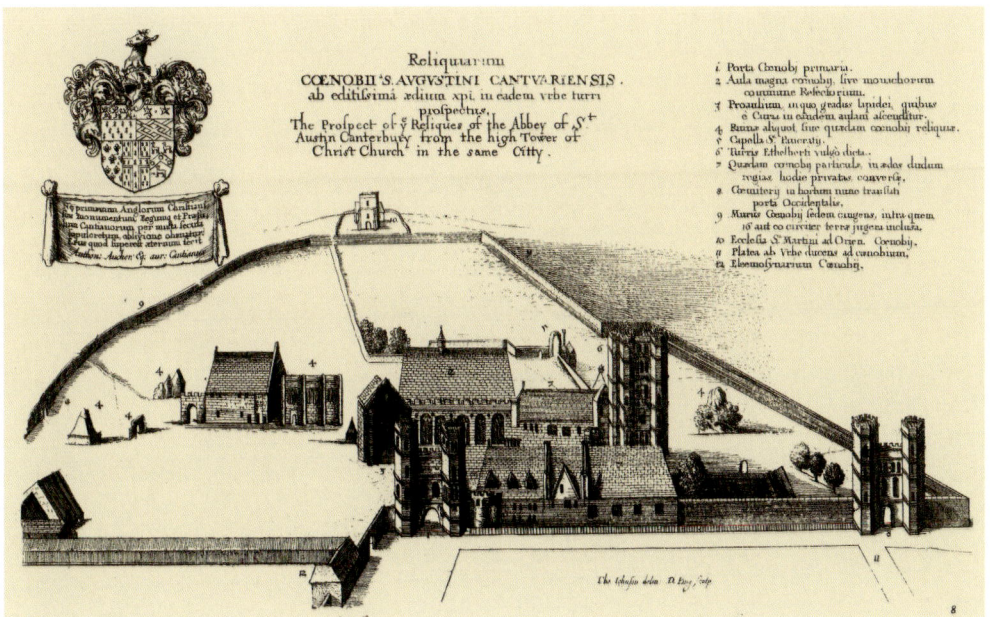

A The painted lead funeral mitre of Abbot John Dygon, 1510

B Gold and cloisonné enamel plaque that adorned a gold-plated silver object; ninth century or earlier

C One of the many tiles from the abbey made locally; this is a late 13th-century example from Tyler Hill in the Forest of Blean

D The 'loving' or 'grace' cup of Abbot John Essex. Such a cup was passed from one person to the other at banquets. Its rim is engraved with a rhyming couplet in Middle English: 'Velcom ze be, dryng for Charite' ('Welcome you be, drink for Charity'). The stem and foot are modern

Collections of the Abbey

Hundreds of objects have been found at the abbey, of which many were deliberately buried with the dead.

As well as the 300 or so surviving books from the abbey, and innumerable pieces of stonework taken after the Suppression and incorporated into buildings in Canterbury and elsewhere, is a significant collection of objects found in the course of excavations.

Some of these are on display in the visitor centre and many more are kept in store at Dover Castle. Other objects, whose origins are not known for certain, may also have come from the abbey; a coconut goblet mounted in silver and now kept at the cathedral is said to have belonged to the last abbot, John Essex (r.1522–38).

Displayed are architectural and sculptural fragments, pavement tiles, funerary items, and objects of stained glass, ivory, bone, ceramic and metal (including personal items such as coins, jewellery, pilgrims' souvenirs and knives). Most of these come from graves and

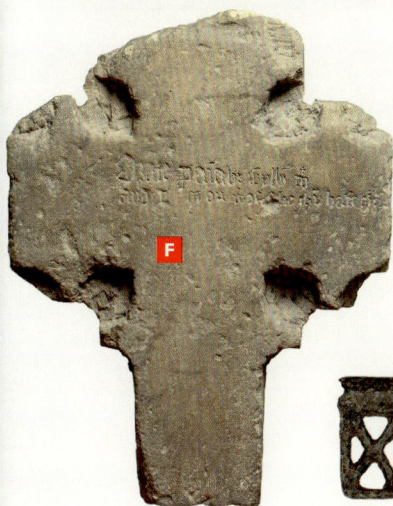

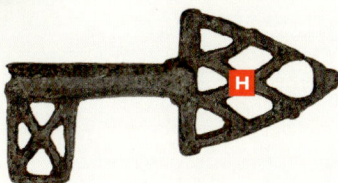

are poignant reminders of the interests and hopes of individual people.

Many fragments of window tracery survive, supporting documentary evidence that the church was given new windows from the late 15th to the early 16th centuries. The brightly painted stones of a delicate Norman arch carved with chevron and dog-tooth ornament testify to the sculptural richness and colour found inside the church.

The solemn funerary items hold a special fascination, for they reveal something of the formality with which the people of the Middle Ages buried their dead. Perhaps the most interesting are the objects found in abbots' graves. They include chalices and patens (small dishes for the Mass wafer), rings, pastoral staves and lead plaques inscribed with epitaphs. The abbey's customary – the detailed book of rules and regulations which governed life at the abbey – states, as was typical, that abbots should be buried with such items; but placed in the graves, equally typically, were base metal imitations of rich pontifical ornaments. In the grave of Abbot John Dygon (r.1497–1510) there was even a leaden mitre, painted to look as though spangled with jewels.

E *Section of a decorated string course depicting a man whose beard is being bitten by beasts. Unusually for its time, it bears the name of its carver: 'Robertus me fecit' (Robert made me); c.1100*

F *Grave marker from the monks' cemetery. Part of the inscription still legible refers to William, a monk*

G *Funerary ring with central glass gem backed with silver foil and textile, originally surrounded by eight little green glass gems; late 14th or 15th century*

H *Elaborate Gothic openwork copper alloy key used for a casket, probably 14th or 15th century*

I *Delicate ivory carving, of unknown purpose, it probably dates from the 16th or 17th century, when the abbey was a private house*

Top: The Great Gate at St Augustine's with the north end of the guest hall beyond it, seen from within the abbey's outer court. The gateway to this court is to the right; watercolour by Jonathan Skelton, 1757

Above: *Portrait of Edward, Lord Wotton, in the late 16th century. by an unknown artist. Wotton bought the abbey from the king in 1612*

The abbot's hall and the watching chamber at its west end (the latter a room from which activities in the hall could be viewed) were incorporated into the palace together with the great kitchen and the Great and Cemetery gates. Ethelbert Tower, the north-west tower of the church, was also incorporated into the palace, as an impressive, picturesque annexe to the new queen's lodgings. The abbot's chapel, too, was retained, thereby preserving the section of the north wall of the nave against which it was built.

Other parts of the abbot's house were demolished and replaced with new chambers. Areas of the precinct were walled off to create a courtyard and spacious royal garden. No monarch ever stayed here for long. This was an occasional rather than a primary royal residence, and was let out to noblemen after 1564.

THE WOTTON AND HALES OCCUPANCIES

In 1612, the site of St Augustine's was purchased from James I (r.1603–25) by Edward (1548–1628), Lord Wotton, an elder statesman in the king's government. Wotton was a Catholic sympathizer (he converted in 1618), and the site's religious history presumably mattered to him. He employed John Tradescant the elder (d.1638), the renowned gardener and collector of curiosities, to lay out three ornamental gardens to the north and east of the palace. These gardens, complete with fountains and statues of mythological figures, were the last addition of any note to the site until the mid 19th century.

When Lord Wotton's second wife and widow, Lady Margaret Wotton, died in 1658, the palace and gardens were inherited by Sir Edward Hales (1645–95), another Roman Catholic convert, and Wotton's great-grandson with his first wife. As a trusted companion of James II (r.1685–8), Hales was present in December 1688 when the defeated king slipped the Great Seal of the realm into the river Thames, a famous act of political mischief. The palace was to remain in the Hales family until 1804–5.

During the Wotton and Hales occupancies, historians began to investigate the abbey site and to make sketches of the ruins. Their work is invaluable, for they drew buildings that are now lost, such as the abbot's chapel and Ethelbert Tower (the last part of which collapsed in 1822). Edward Hales's descendants let out some of the buildings and sold off small parcels of land. The chamber over the Great Gate was at some point used for cockfighting, and the gate later housed a brewery. In the 18th and 19th centuries an inn called The Old Palace occupied the monastic guesthouse on the south side of the gate. A poorhouse was built within the lay cemetery in 1793 and a new gaol opened in the same quarter in 1808. By that date, the site was ripe for urban development, which would have obliterated the visible medieval remains.

ST AUGUSTINE'S COLLEGE AND STATE GUARDIANSHIP

Fortunately for posterity, most of the abbey site was bought in the mid 1840s by Sir Alexander James Beresford Hope, a politician, author and art collector. Hope recognized the outstanding historical importance of St Augustine's but initially had no clear plan for the site. Before long, however, he had formed a partnership with Edward Coleridge, a master at Eton, to found a missionary college. St Augustine's College operated from 1848 until 1947, after which its buildings were let to the King's School.

Below: Portrait of Sir Alexander James Beresford Hope, probably in the 1860s, some years after he bought the remains of St Augustine's Abbey

Bottom: Copy of a sketch by George Cooper of Ethelbert's Tower on 23 October 1822, the day before its surviving remnants were finally demolished to avoid a dangerous collapse

Above: This photograph of the Great Gate was taken in June 1950. It shows the extensive damage to the building caused by air raids in 1942, during the Second World War

Above right: Excavations at the abbey in the early 20th century

Below: View of the abbey remains today, from the south-east

Hope, who was highly knowledgeable about architecture, employed William Butterfield to design the College buildings. Butterfield, then only 30, was to become one of England's great Gothic Revival architects. Working closely with his patron, he designed smart, two-storey buildings with split-flint facings and red-tile roofs. To make it stand out, the library to be built on the site of the abbot's hall (by this time probably a ruin) was given freestone facing and tall windows with Gothic tracery. The work exposed some of the site's medieval remains and gave rise to further archaeological investigation, which lasted until the 1980s and exposed the core monastic buildings, together with many peripheral ones.

In 1938 the Office of Works took over guardianship of the site, thereby establishing public access. This arrangement continues today, with English Heritage as guardian of the publicly accessible southern section of the abbey site, which is owned by the St Augustine's Foundation. In 1989 UNESCO declared St Augustine's Abbey a World Heritage Site.